I dedicate this book to
Nicole, Ava, and John
who inspire me every day,
with all the love in my heart.

TURN YOUR

LIFE

All the best,

W

7-17-14

INSIGHT OUT

Wendy Di Bella

OPEN THIS BOOK TO ANY RANDOM PAGE

NOTICE IT IS NOT SO RANDOM AT ALL

Published by

wendyland publishing

ISBN 978-0-9915816-0-3

Cover design by Brenda DeRose
Interior layout by Jonathan Gullery

Printed on ♻ recycled paper in the United States of America

Acknowledgments

A big THANK YOU to God.

I would also like to acknowledge and express my deepest gratitude to:

My mother, father and sister for a lifetime of encouragement, inspiration, love, and support.

My in-laws, for being so generously loving and supportive.

My friends, for bringing so much joy and fun to my life.

Nevine, of Katonah Yoga, my teacher and friend, for yoga that enriches my life beyond words and words that enrich my life beyond yoga.

My supportive, wonderful yoga community, for providing an abundance of great teachers, great students, and great friends. With special loving thanks to Joanna, Brenda L, Harriet, Diane, and Brenda D.

Matt, for being a truly gifted and skilled coherent healer.

Last but certainly not least, YOU, the reader, for being open to connect with the special gift within you that fulfills your life and enriches our world.

Note From Author

There I was—I just turned thirty and was excited about it. Then, BAM! Something changed. I was distracted from my usual carefree, "believe it and achieve it" kind of self. Depressed? No, I don't get depressed. Anxious? No, I'm as calm as a cucumber—but there I was—surprised to admit that I was both depressed and anxious, and asking God, "Why?"

I sought help but realized immediately that the prescribed pills and the conventional methods I had found were not helping me to overcome the feelings and experiences that would hold me back at times from fully participating in life. In fact, the few prescriptions I tried dulled my senses, producing the opposite effect of what was natural to me.

I became determined to get to the root cause of these scary and unnatural feelings that were holding me back from fully living in the present moment, enjoying my family, friends, and life. I got into yoga, which to this day, enriches my life beyond words. Other alternative healing methods have also helped. One particular energy healing session that I went into very nonchalantly, actually changed my life that very day. I started writing. The words flowed effortlessly, and the articulations that came out spoke to me in phrases that I was hearing for the first time, even though I had spent a lifetime living them. A few weeks later I realized I was writing a book, or rather, a book was writing itself through me.

This is how God answered me.

CONTENTS

Articulations are works of art created to provide access to unlimited growth potential through awareness and insight on taking action and participating in your own well-being.

Articulations

Dialog that emerges and erupts to incite,
you to turn your life, experience more delight.
Rotating on your axis point,
with freedom and movement, using a universal joint.
Past occurrences used to learn from,
liberation's clue provided within, a breadcrumb.
No more than that is ever needed,
articulations, a simple necklace, beautifully beaded.
An autobiography for all social classes,
appealing to and helping heal the masses.
Using the information to live a life fulfilled and good,
be your own interpreter, so easily understood.
Exposing a healthy high functioning autonomic reaction,
revealing the full benefits and insights of the laws of attraction.

(ART = work produced - I = self - CUL = a passage with
access only at one end - ATIONS = process, action or condition)

Preface

Well there comes a time when you're ready to be free
and I found the light that eluded me.
I watch myself on a movie reel,
and the storyline seems so unreal.

I was a prisoner who is now free
from a death-row sentence pardoning me.
When you think you're taking your very last breath,
you find rebirth within that death.

It was hard to see the light ahead
because I had moments filled with dread.
All of the things that possessed me,
prevented me from being free
not feeling high, not feeling grand—
this whole perspective in my hand.

When you lose your love and lose your light;
when there's no more will to stand and fight;
the highs and lows spin you like a top
that suddenly halts and you take a flop.

When the love and pain, pain and love,
shoot through your veins like an addictive drug,
you cannot smile when you're wearing a frown;
you can't be happy when you're feeling down.

Now from the dark I see the light.
I moved to the light and looked back down.
In my rearview mirror I wore a Burger King crown,
paper thin and boring brown.
My royalty was dim and gray
with small deposits every day.
I learned the truth I'm writing now

to state and make a royal vow.
To live the light I know exists
to enjoy lifelong living bliss
to share the truth that I have learned
if you want to heal you must be burned.
My experiences have made me see
I've embraced them all, I'm healed and free…

SECTION I

Insight 1

Detoxing

Quiet

Silence

Detoxing

When detox mode is what you're in
and icy chills creep up your skin,
when stomach pangs are sharp and tight
and you don't know if you'll get through the night.
When feeling good seems far away
but something tells you watch and pray.
Letting go of toxic fumes
regardless of the drug that looms.
Consuming pills from prescriptions,
or maybe shooting worse addictions,
or maybe it's a different kind
of toxic substance from the mind.
It matters not what starts your trouble
detoxing is a lonely bubble.
But as your substance does release
you will know what it is to live in peace.

Wendy DiBella

Quiet

It's quiet now. The rain has passed.
the subtle silence seems to last.
Still damp from water, wet night's dew,
my thinking mind has less to chew.
I dare to dream the bliss I crave
from times I've lived in my dark cave.
The love I knew, the joy of life
keeps me waiting out my strife.
The water drip so clean and clear
in subtle silence you can hear.
The cherry stem that's still attached
has safety of connected batch.
The disconnected water hose
just drips or leaks and spills its gold.
I'll hold on longer; I can see
there is still hope; I will be free.

Silence

Silence speaks much louder than all
and the room that it gives is so wide and so tall.
There is no pain within that space;
it exists to heal the human race.
It is only a place awaiting to know
that you have arrived and are ready to show
kind words of love and gestures of light,
embracing natural sounds in the day and the night.
But first you must know the experience of peace
before you can hear what silence speaks.

Wendy DiBella

Insight 2

Thoughts

Mind Chatter

Volcanos

Thoughts

Were you looking for me?
To speak your sadness or glee?
Interrupting any time you please,
did you like the power of making me freeze
in my tracks when you talk
in my life, when you stalk?
Just a warning, I've watched you too.
Did you notice that I've stalked you?
I think you should know I saw you there
you had so much to say with so little care.
So I decided I've heard enough of your banter.
However, I do appreciate your intellectual candor.
I've upped our dialog, integrated positive belief,
connected to full healing, greatness and relief.
Don't worry, I won't completely cut you out
when I can use you, I'll give you a shout.
Until that time, so long, bon jour.
For your incessantness, I found a cure.

Mind Chatter

I held on clenching—oh so tight—
to colliding thoughts, in a cosmic fight
that kept me trapped in outer space
with inner thoughts I couldn't face.
When the cork could hold no more,
it popped and exploded with all I had bore.
Now the thoughts have space to roam
and settle in their proper home
of teaching others that their pain
shall not be endured in vain.
If you've had a similar blight
then connect with my thoughts, bring yourself to the light.

Volcanos

Volcanos sit for many years
quiet sometimes, filled with tears
from energies so very near,
teasing, taunting it's eruption fear.
But if a volcano denies its nature
to erupt and explode and create some danger,
then how will it ever know the peace
of such a very grand release
and fulfill what it's meant to do:
Just spew.

Wendy DiBella

Insight 3

Teacher

Dyslexia

Teacher

School was not such a friend of mine;
I was dyslexic but didn't know it at the time.
It was a challenge just to read;
feeling stupid made me bleed
out all my confidence in scholastic regard.
Compensatory strategies became real hard.
Teacher's pet I was not
so quietly I just sat in one spot.
Paralyzed, sometimes I would feel
that my shortcomings would be revealed.
So I did what I knew best:
sat in the back, blended in with the rest.
Learning did not excite me;
I felt such a lack of competency.
Until the day my spirit was ready
my teacher appeared and my learning grew steady.
Her compassion and insight was so binding
she gave me skills and tools for unwinding.
She gave herself so honestly
and showed me how great I can be.
I know now it's not about what you're taught;
it's about what you learn when you're not overwrought
with gross misconceptions of what's smart and what's not.
A great teacher helps you untie those knots.
This teacher of mine that made things so clear
her name is Nevine; she's a great pioneer.

Wendy DiBella

Dyslexia

Dyslexics have a special gift:
their minds paint pictures, they're very swift.
Difficulty in reading is only because
words with no pictures create space and pause
the reader from understanding everything.
The, *its*, *ands* and *buts* do not a picture bring.
These holes in the story leaves way too much room
for misinterpretation and comprehensionless gloom.
Since a picture tells 1,000 words,
words with no pictures cut a story by two thirds.
The story looks a lot like Swiss cheese
to the dyslexic reader who is reading to please
the conventional systems put into place
to uniformly teach the human race.
But now it's time for that system to know
what *it* needs to comprehend to help *itself* grow.
It's not about redundantly reading and repeating;
it's understanding sight words like the salutation in the greeting.
It's creating a relationship with every lower- and upper-case letter
that alone allows the person to start reading better.
It's balancing orientation of the dyslexic mind's eye
so that speed and comprehension can permanently apply.
Most of all it's teaching dyslexics to paint a picture for each word
so every story is whole and complete, all knowledge is transferred.
It's important to know that dyslexics are *not* of average intelligence;
they are way way above; their mind looks for the relevance.
They must be told that how they learn and see
is a language-based difficulty, not a disability.
In truth, they're highly advanced and think brilliantly,
which is one of the reasons their mind holds the key
to bringing our world inspired inventions, beauty, art, and fun.
Albert Einstein and Walt Disney used their dyslexia to get it done.
I hope I've helped *you* paint a pretty picture in *your* mind
of how dyslexic people are a gift to all mankind.

Insight 4

Mind's Eye

Unraveling

Whirlwind

Uncovering

Mind's Eye

Knowing it, thinking it,
confronting and revealing it.
Provocative, mysterious,
utterly delirious.
Knowing that the thoughts you think
can lead you to the utter brink.
Your vision takes the things you see
and makes them your reality.
Cajoling you, seducing you,
to keep you in the loop de loo,
rhetoric; a magic stick,
knowing now that you've been tricked.
Holding on until it's safe
and negative thinking you erase.

Wendy DiBella

Whirlwind

Lost then found
I watched it spin around.
Pulled in, got out—
it made me wanna shout.
Then I was silenced by the pain
of moving through it again.
Let this be
final freedom for me.

Unraveling

What's this flow that's minding me?
Maybe its unwinding me?
But not the me that's woven right
just the parts wound too tight.
Is there a point to this all?
Or just the journey as most like to call?
Who is listening to my flow?
Or is it just for me to know?
I didn't know I knew these words
I hadn't studied all of these verbs.
So from where is my information cast
and will it move me forward from my past?
Articulation *is* what I do
but none of this is what I thought I knew.

Wendy DiBella

Uncovering

I'm starting to uncover who I really am
and realize it may conflict with my original plan.
I don't know if everyone will like the new me.
What I mean by that is, will my family?
For so long I thought I knew who I was
and my recent findings have disproved it because
there are so many new things I can now see
since uncovered; there's a change in me.
In this process of holding it all together
I'm really riding out all kinds of weather
with stormy days, and sunshine too;
the back and forth my mind does chew.
The sun plays hide and seek, when out from behind the cloud
it unveils and uncovers, like removing a shroud.
I watch all this happen as if it's not me
waiting with faith, patiently.

Insight 5

Sex

Money

Success

Sex

Why are we so surprised to see
sex scenes in every big screen movie?
It's in everything we do—
it's in every part of you.
It's not exactly what most think—
it's the perfect fit, the connecting link.
In all the world it does reflect
these interpretations to be correct,
be it a hand in a fist or an eye in socket,
a ball in a joint or something in your pocket,
two hands clapping that create a sound,
the connection of two brings a third around.
The purpose of sex, it's essence, creation,
a functional use of each component's vibration.
In the mathematical equation of sex,
one + one equals three; it's the fourth dimensional triplex.

Wendy DiBella

Money

When your goal is to have money,
it laughs and thinks you're very funny.
"Where should I go?" the money asks,
"You haven't given me a task."
"I'm currency so I can easily flow
to anyplace you'd like me to go."
"Tell me why you call to me?
Is it so you can live life free?
Is it so you can have some fun
and live it up on the beach in the sun?
Is it to fuel the career of your choice?
Is it to take singing lessons and enhance your voice?
Is it to buy your vacation house?
Or have a romantic dinner with your spouse?
Just give me a reason and I'll be there,
the only place you can't call me from is despair."

When you're inspired by your passion,
money shows up in easy fashion.
When you're living the life you love,
money connects to you from above.
When you do what makes you happy,
money comes fast-paced and snappy.
When you believe in your goals and dreams,
money flows in endless streams.
When you have faith and remove all fear,
money arrives because your mind is clear.
When your relationship with money is on positive terms,
it comes to prove you should believe, your every dream it reaffirms.

You can't call money from despair.
It won't hear you; it doesn't live there.

Success

Flow with the best of them;
roll with the rest of em.
Bounce when you fall;
connect when you call.
Turn on a dime;
manipulate time.
Live in the now;
take a sincere bow.

Wendy DiBella

Insight 6

Power

Kindness

Forgiveness

Non-Forgiveness

/Beyond-Forgiveness

Power

Plugged in, energies in charge,
currents flowing, steady and large.
Using energy efficiently,
living self-sufficiently.
Creating magic, having skill,
attaching goals to your will.
Having patience and a vision,
executing quick decision.
Giving only from abundance,
growing wise from life's redundance.
Influence and skilled control,
maintaining a powerful, happy soul.

Kindness

Kindness should not be your main goal;
power is what you want to control.
When you have power you are able to do
greater things for yourself and others, too.
So many people lead with their heart
assuming that sets them to a great start,
but in truth it's power that enables you to perform
larger acts of kindness, making lives transform.
People lose a lot of energy if they lie and steal
or spend too much time trying to wheel and deal.
The most powerful people do not waste their time;
they use what they have to help themselves and others climb.
Put yourself back in the control tower
so that all acts of kindness come from your power.

Forgiveness

To forgive does not mean that you have to forget;
You can't erase the past event or regret.
What you can do is take back your power
that you gave up when you became bitter and sour.
To forgive is something that benefits you;
would you forgive all, if you knew this was true?
Forgiveness begins when you separate
the event from the feeling that makes you hate.
Knowing we don't all see eye to eye,
people's actions only reflect how they deal and get by.
Usually it's not personal to you;
how they act and behave is their internal view.
When you hear or see something from only your perspective,
remember that one angle is very subjective.
Before fast assumptions are made and regarded
separate past occurrences from which your mind is bombarded.
Look at the instance that you resent
and ask the individual if bad intention was meant.
If they answer, yes, thank them and let it go right there;
by showing themselves, they saved you future despair.
If the answer is an honest no,
in that moment believe them and let it go.
Some relationships provide only fool's gold,
so make wise decisions about which ones you will hold.
You must also forgive yourself for not knowing
that you may have had relationships that were slowing
you down from doing different things or being in a better place
that you can now access with forgiveness's grace.

Wendy DiBella

Non-Forgiveness/ Beyond-Forgiveness

Not having to forgive is one level higher
than forgiveness itself, for it does not require
your blessing, forgiving something that was done
by yourself or another, for blame or shame there is none.
Nothing was done that requires you to excuse
just moments passed that reflected some views.
They had no relevance to your state of being;
you remain full and whole, non-forgiveness is freeing.
You realize no one or nothing can take that away—
no specific circumstances required to complete you or your day.
You observe, not absorb, the events taking place;
when something occurs you just give it some space.
In quick time you set up your world to reflect
a life beyond forgiveness, filled with love and respect.

Insight 7

Denial

Acceptance

Decisiveness

Denial

Denial is a devious emotion
that carries much weight in a poisonous potion.
For healing's properties to be formed
denial must be removed and you be informed,
that you are much greater than you think you are
and have power that can take you very far.
Denying that you've tried to take control
of other's lives, while their energy you stole
whether kids or parents or someone else who
you've wanted to help or have them love you
so you unconsciously took on their damage or pain.
But you must give it back; over other's lives you can't reign.
Also they need it to be complete.
In this world they have to stand on their own two feet,
and it doesn't benefit you, not one little bit.
It's an extra layer of bulk on you that will never fit.
Also, retrieve what loved ones may have taken from you,
on the occasions when you appeared upset or blue.
Take back your energy that makes you complete
so you too can stand on your own two feet.
When it's only your stuff with which you have to deal
it's easy to accept, handle, and heal.
The first step in revealing denial starts right here;
the rest will be easy and in quick time appear.
All you have to do to ensure your success
is believe, retrieve, and from your heart address.
To see what *you're* denying, notice where you're stewing;
your denial's hidden in what you accuse others of doing.
Denial is the root of the main block
that prevents someone from changing, taking personal stock.
Denial is simply resistance in disguise.

Wendy DiBella

Resistance is exhausting, non-beneficial, and unwise.
Once denial is gone you can easily do it:
overcome, heal, and get quickly through it.
When there is no denial what is left in its place?
It's called acceptance and with it, everything you can embrace.

Acceptance

Within acceptance lives joy, peace, and freedom.
It holds all your desires, dreams, and wisdom.
It waits until you're ready to let it in
and showers you with grace so you can begin
to have all the things you've dreamed of and then some.
All you need do initially is give it a breadcrumb.
It has the master key to every door
opening to goodness and letting go of things you bore.
Simply accepting that you may not accept
is an easy, important very first step.
The more you accept, the more accepts you,
just as you are, I promise it's true.

Decisiveness

Yes or no, no or yes?
Am I or am I not doing my very best?
Aligned in three
"yes" or "no" must be.
Thoughts, feelings, actions
don't serve as fractions.
Combining these three
is a holy trinity.
Choose "yes" or "no"; either is fine
so long as in the trinity they align.
An example would be an ice cream treat
if you decide you want it, and feel good while you eat
then you will benefit from having that cone
unless you eat it with guilt and groan.
If your mind says yes but your feeling says NO,
and your action is yes, no good could bestow.
For every decision that you align all three
the choice, each time, will serve you splendidly.

Insight 8

Death

Loss

Growth

Death

Nothing ever really dies
in space and time it moves and glides.
In and out like a revolving door
with every turn you fully restore.
The universe always makes sure
each individual is loved and cared for.

Wendy DiBella

Loss

Some things must go so there is space
for new things to come in and take their place.
Most things are lost so others can be found;
this is the way the world goes around.
Appreciating and enjoying what you have today
makes you feel fulfilled and accepting if or when that something goes
away.

Growth

Growth is when you take the things
you've had all along and give them wings.
Like giving a seed, soil, water, and sun
creating a flower from where there was none.
It's not taking something and making it better;
it's complete transformation, yarn becomes a sweater.
Caterpillars cocoon to nearly die
to live at their highest vibration as a butterfly.
Changing something simple to a more complex form
unfolding and ironing of wrinkles that by the object are worn.
Before a flowers grows it knows the dark and the blight;
once it passes soil's edge, it sees, feels, and lives the light.

Wendy DiBella

Insight 9

Belief

Matter

Participate

Belief

Are you ready to believe
that you truly can achieve
what you want, what you need
and bring it to yourself with lightning speed?
Will you take that very step
that will help you redirect
your visions and your goals
and soothe your achy soul?
Be connected to all that is good,
live the joyful life that you should.

Matter

The matter that makes up your life
from brilliant times to awful strife,
from highest health to ailing pain:
knowing from where it comes will be your gain.
You may think that it's genetic,
but in truth it's just kinetic.
Energy and currents move in you
and every single thing you do
when you clear out all your blocks
and flow with life like water over rocks.
Then DNA plays its best role
and supports your healthy, happy soul.
Your history is not to blame
nor relatives that cause you shame.
Your present state is what makes up
the elixir in your golden cup.

Participate

Participating is the way
you become a part of each new day.
To participate in your own health,
is how to achieve ultimate wealth.
To participate in having fun
is how a happy life is done.
To participate in being forgiving
is how to have a life worth living.
To participate in healing pain
is how to remove stress and strain.
To participate in your own success
is how to ensure you make progress.
To participate in being present
is how to ensure your time's well spent.
To participate in gaining power
is how to have energy every hour.
To participate in something bigger
is how to live your life with vigor.
To participate in your well being
is how a great life you're guaranteeing.

Insight 10

Pain

Agitation

Addiction

Pain

The pain of striving to get upstream
against the current is no one's dream.
The pain of physically feeling hurt
can steal your attention and your mind divert.
The pain of emotional *dis*comfort and un*ease*
is the root cause of all dis-ease.
The pain of not trusting, not having belief
is the cause of feeling all peril and grief.
The pain of mixing thoughts of money with fear
makes your goals and visions very unclear.
The pain of a shorted-out system of nerves
interferes with currency, and all that it serves.
The pain of feeling lusterless or lacking
creates mind chatter, keeps the brain racking.
The pain of a thought that doesn't match your feeling
confuses your spirit and sends your mind reeling.
The pain of fighting to convince or convert
is the ego's means to bitterly assert.
The pain of not having quite enough love
crowds free space and is uncharacteristic of,
God, which is love, and love which is space
there is no pain once you embrace
all the abundance of life's luster
that fills *your* life when you become a real truster.
Removing suppressed emotion sets you free,
feelings and thoughts align happily.
Using affirmations, focused concentration,
eating healthy, exercising for energy calibration.
The pain is your map, in it you read
which direction to go, what signs to heed.
Pursue methods of healing, completely different from how
and what you've spent time and money on till now.
Acceptance of truth, being one to see
the brilliance of the universe, your life and thee.

Wendy DiBella

Pain is your friend, it has love for you;
it only stays around to help steer you through.
When you don't need guidance, it will bid you adieu,
and you will be rid of the pain you once knew.
It's important to know that life uses measure
for the level of pain, turned, becomes your level of pleasure.
Oh, the love and joy that you have and share
when you're pain free. I'll see you there.

Agitation

Life's agitation aggravates to move
people to places so they can improve.
A pearl is created by agitation of sand.
The pressure on coal puts a diamond on your hand.
A caterpillar nears death to become its highest self;
the agitation in your life is for your betterment and health.

Addiction

Addictions are habits you feel forced to do
regardless of the consequences to you.
Cravings that are so intense,
"I can't help it," is just a pretense
but helping "it" is what you end up doing
until the time you stop pursuing
those things that keep you down and out
and the related issues they bring about.
Some of these habitual addictions
are drugs, alcohol, food, and unhealthy convictions.
Any daily habit that you may do
unconsciously, does not benefit you.
Even brushing your teeth without conscious thought
allows areas to be missed where bacteria gets caught.
Bring unconscious actions to your awareness,
expose and strip them down to their bareness.
Once these subjects are brought to light,
take back stock in yourself, exercise your preemptive right.

(Preemptive right = The right to acquire new issue, undiluted shares of
stock)

Insight 11

Alignment

Effortless

Art/Work

Alignment

Aligning is when two or more things correlate.
Views, wants, and desires add up and equate
to similar parallel thoughts that correspond
on many subjects of which both are fond.
Everyone wants to be well-adjusted
and line up with others that they feel are trusted.
Take a close look at people's opinions you value;
calculate those that measure up and which you should revalue.
What and whom you align with will determine for sure
the experiences of your life and your ability to procure.

Effortless

Effortless effort,
also know as Wu Wei
is being in complete harmony with events of your day.
The opposite of thinking, talking, or planning,
it's obtaining gold without even panning.
It's a very natural, uncontrived way
to experience lightheartedness, live in a bright ray.
Just like the way the planet revolves
or your body's own health it resolves.
It's like the way a flower will grow
with no effort on its part and yet steal the show,
or the way that enough pressure and time
can create a flawless diamond in a mine.
Have you ever had something come right to you
without working hard or detailing it through?
Have you ever felt the ease of doing something hard
like running for miles that felt like a yard?
This is the way your life is meant to run;
"trying easier" is so much more fun.
Look at the things that are effortless for you
and infuse and use them in everything you do.

Art/Work

Not a word was written here, with force or contrive.

No aspect of this book stemmed from the need to survive.

From no point of desperation did any of this evolve.

It was quite the opposite that provided such resolve.

Every word and sentence was formed with the greatest of ease,

from present moment, with grateful thoughts,

the whole thing was a breeze.

If at any moment my mind did start to wander,

I closed my book and let it go; this task I would not squander.

Any work of art that is created has a muse.

I stayed connected to my inspiration with open-minded views.

Any artist's work can be worth a mint,

it must reflect the best of you, and on the world imprint.

Insight 12

Love

Hate

Negative/Positive

Love

Love is the highest vibrational level
in your happy, joyful excitement you revel.
Seratonin percolates and bubbles right through;
love always shows off the best version of you.
In its vast and many unbridled forms
your view of life will and does transform.
Lightning lifting up your soul
strikes you and takes all control.
When overwhelmed with desire and attraction
accompanied with a magnetic fraction
that's pulling towards it's completing piece,
embraced in a kiss it will increase,
the dreamy, can't-eat, excitement felt
when romance is the love you're dealt.
The love for a child is the strongest kind
of euphoric joy that permeates your mind.
So much love is available to you—
everyday choose to love something new.
People, job, sports, and hobbies
are just some areas where love lobbies.
Creation is the driving force.
It is not meant to be reigned in; set it free like a wild horse.

Hate

Hate is the lowest vibrational level
in anger and unhappiness it makes you revel.
Hormones like cortisol build up in your body
lowering functionality, making workmanship shoddy.
Simmering, stewing in a big hot mess
going to extremes, experiencing stress.
To release yourself from hate's harsh hold
know that its basis is twofold:
What comes out, reflects what's in
from inner turmoil hatred does begin.
Negative things you project on to another,
are positive qualities about yourself that you smother.
To stop the anger that you express out,
unveil from inside your inner self-doubt.
What you despise that boils your blood,
reveals where you drag yourself through mud.
You're the only one who suffers from your hate,
the way you feel about yourself is how to others you relate.
When in all aspects of yourself you have confidence and love,
any and all hate in your heart you will be free of.

Negative/Positive

Negative and positive electrical fields
determine the experience a person yields.
In science we learn negative energy charges in,
this can become an overcrowded reaction, wherein
limitations are reached as to what one can take
and our bodies we certainly cannot forsake.
Positive energy always charges out,
releasing and creating space, no doubt.
But it's not safe to empty your entire gas tank
and always keep plenty of money in your bank.
Also, you don't want a false positive;
you'll have a false measure of what you have to give.
About these polarities you must be smart;
they affect many areas, especially the heart.
On either side of each energy's coin
is where opposite energies can conjoin.
Two "like" charges will only repel,
but a positive and negative connect real well.
One lets in and the other lets out,
allowing balanced flow and movement throughout.
Thomas Edison may have brought us light
but a balanced, flowing life *you* must ignite.

Wendy DiBella

Insight 13

Fear

Anxiety

Depression

Quitting

Fear

Fear is such a tumultuous trap;
it is like a mystery to unwrap
because the problem is fear itself,
not the various reasons you've stored on a shelf.
When fear's siren starts to sound,
your scared subconscious takes you down.
Taking on the shape of darker things,
fear attaches to you with imaginary strings.
It can resemble any form
and grow in strength as you get worn.
To isolate and remove its confusion
you must be able to see past the illusion.
You can divide and conquer it
first, don't trust the feeling in your stomach's pit.
Know that you've been giving it permission
to perform for you, with only brief intermissions.
When you remember that you run the show
you can face this emotion and let it go.
Once you confront it, you'll get fast relief;
it never had the power to give you any grief.
It was you all along who attached yourself to it,
remove all cords and shut down its wit.
Tap on yourself until the fear is detached
from the thought of which it was originally hatched.
Tapping instructions are provided within;
it works so great, share it with your next of kin.
Fear has been playing with you for too long,
but now you can be the smart one, that is so strong.
You've always had the option to choose faith over fear;
both cannot exist within the same sphere.
I know all this because I had feared, too
but fear no more, you now know what to do.

*See *Tapping*, page 189

Wendy DiBella

Anxiety

Anxiety is a fast-forward button,
thoughts of the future that come on real sudden.
Once it is pushed it all happens so fast,
like a sudden uncontrolled scary blast,
a rush that speeds up your heart,
and shortens breath right from the start.
If you want to pause, stop, or rewind,
you have to sneak up on it from behind.
Slow down your breathing, start to unwind,
bring your mind to the present time.
Then, forward fold while sitting on a chair,
put your knees in your armpits, take twenty slow breaths there.
Next, take a look at what's on your mind,
be not afraid, this will work every time.
Look at what your mind has to say,
face the thoughts that scare you today.
Tap on them to separate the emotions from
the thoughts themselves, get out of the doldrums.
No real power do they hold;
simply remove them from the fold
of the crease that was made and reflects in real time,
the new patterns you create to finally feel fine.

*See *Tapping*, page 189

Depression

Thoughts of the past trigger depression;
it's degenerative disease is regression.
How it works is, its sadness holds you
pretending to comfort and console, too.
It's very convincing when you feel alone;
you believe it's your friend you just called on the phone.
Well, let me tell you, it is no friend of yours.
It smothers and stifles and tangles you in cords.
The easiest way to just let it go
is know that you can look for a glow.
A spark of light that can lead the way
and bring your mind to the present day.
If old thoughts have something more to say
send them off into that ray
of light that you have found in you
that lets you pull yourself right through.
Allow each thought to go in peace
so all depression can and does cease.
*Tap on yourself to move these thoughts through
so you can live in the present and know this is true.
When the present process of life is what you're immersed in,
you're over depression, you win.

*See *Tapping*, page 189

Wendy DiBella

Quitting

I never really felt before
the pain of quitting, sealing shut a door,
something that was joyfully started
but as time went on, joy left, departed.
Why begin to never finish?
Why was belief and joy gone, diminished?
For prior to this all my effort's reward
was bountiful with no discord.
In that time of loneliness and loss
under my feet I saw the moss.
Standing stiffly, heels dug in
wanting to move, but stuck like a pin,
wanting to cry, but dried up inside,
wanting to accept, but in the way my pride,
wanting to let go, but too strong was my hold,
wanting to fly, but weighted with scold,
wanting to know, but scared of the truth,
wanting to have drive, but old was my youth,
wanting to appreciate, but didn't feel deserving,
wanting to do good, but needed energy for serving,
wanting to start over, but didn't trust I could do it,
wanting to forget, but wasn't yet through it,
wanting to feel great, but didn't even feel good,
wanting to be myself, but didn't think I should,
wanting to not go deep, but deep is where I lived,
wanting to live up high, but permission to myself I didn't give.
I wanted the Midas touch that I once had,
but that requires inner vibrance, not feeling sad,
I wanted to be loved, believed in, and respected,
but had no confidence these views could be resurrected.
I knew that wanting was holding me back
from not feeling self-destructive and lack.

Quitting's glass is always half empty
while letting go is always filled with plenty.
I fully and truly finally did let go;
abundance is now, once again, what I know.

Wendy DiBella

Insight 14

Blame

Bitterness

Awareness

Blame

I finally heard everything said.
I finally learned from all the dread.
I had insisted I knew it all
and blamed myself for every fall.
The blame hidden within you
takes control while you have no clue.
No longer will I play the game
of right and wrong with it and shame.
It's time for me to move on now
to let it go today, right now.
I removed the cords that before I kept
that made me sad. I often wept,
blame and me at every point
were connected by an artificial joint.
It told me, "All the problems were because of you."
I now recuse myself, for it was untrue.
Thinking I was supported by blame
but seeing now that was just its game,
I have already let go of the hurt and pain
by removing its needle, I cleaned my vein.
It's revealing to really look back now
I met it halfway in; that is shocking—wow!
I won't meet it halfway anymore.
I'm so far out it can't touch my core.
I don't enable it to tell me lies.
I see clearly now through my own eyes.
I no longer accept some tethered threads
as insulting gifts while indignity spreads.
I know that me being all the way out
will help others to also wake up and shout,
"I did pass the test. I see it all now,
experiencing disconnect had been my vow.
I can move on; my experience is over,
I've turned a new leaf; I am a four leaf clover.

Wendy DiBella

Faith, belief, love, and good luck
are my new embodiment, I am no longer stuck."
I believe this fate can bestow on you
good luck and success in pulling through.
As for me, I've given back everyone else's energy.
I no longer take theirs on, just mine for me.
From this moment I yield in all good power.
I am full, whole, and complete; I am a new bright tower.

Bitterness

A tightness in your gut and view
giving a sourly, raged review
a sigh, a sink, a slap, a slope
a personal, predisposed hanging rope:
My teacher taught me bitterness is life's greatest defeat.
It's putting in great effort and still getting beat,
contrary to how pursuing goals with efficiency
gets you what you seek, because of proficiency.
Happiness then stems as your efforts reward
and there is no bitterness or any discord.
No need to be bitter, upset, or blue;
all that's required is to see this is true.
Use less effort and more efficiency, to invite
magnanimity, contentment, goodwill, and delight.

Wendy DiBella

Awareness

She is the truth; you're now awake;
she reveals to you where you've been fake.
She gives you drive and motivation
to make great choices; she is revelation.
The clouds she lifts open to blue skies.
She is success instead of tries.
She proves to you, you're a very good soul
keeping you grounded is your gain and her goal.
You're healed and happy and doing the right thing;
loving, goodness to your life she'll always bring.

Insight 15

Vow

Marriage

Disconnected

Reconnecting

Realigned

Vow

We took a vow, we took a chance
to go through life, a paired romance.
I don't recall having even one fight.
For the first fifteen years, it was fun, smooth, and light.
Then we hit a unseen bump in the road;
we stopped to check it out, we got towed,
taken to a place off our route
of happiness and love's pursuit.
We had to take care of the damage from the bump
frustrated by the detour, we were in a slump.
After some time the mending was done;
we were back on our way, a new journey begun.
New roads ahead, past left behind;
this journey was of a circular kind.
We traveled back to things we knew before
but in a different setting, on a new shore
a higher plain, but right at sea level.
Now gazing at each other we could smile and revel
in the fact that we still do belong together
and reaffirm how much we're birds of a feather.
We had a breakdown but not one regret,
our breakthrough kept our vow and *us* a well-paired duet.

Wendy DiBella

Marriage

We used to meet on every plane
with love and joy within our veins.
We used to hike to mountaintops
so energized we wouldn't stop.
We used to go on awesome dates
and couldn't help but stay out late.
We used to dream about our lives
and take each day with happy stride.
One day it came to just not be
this gleeful happy friendship with me.
Important matters quickly changed,
views of life were rearranged.
We started taking different paths,
the potholes drained our bubble baths.
We fought to share our points and views
but that didn't work so we dropped clues.
Rolling eyes or glancing stares
just made worse our demanding dares.
We knew that we had to start
doing something from the heart.
We knew that we had to be,
back to happy, fun, and free
but if just wanting were enough
we'd already have back all that stuff.
Realigning our goals and vision became the key,
to our happily ever after or setting each other free.

Disconnected

I am so mad at him right now:
he won't "go there" no way, no how.
It keeps on smacking him in the face:
my words, my words, he can't embrace.
I feel like I have lost all credibility,
and he doesn't seem to have any humility.
According to him he can do no wrong
and I'm a pretend shrink that's annoyingly strong.
He's the one pretending that it's not true
that we're disconnected and it makes us both blue.
He does not see that sometimes I feel low;
it is a place he does not go,
but I see him way up high
looking down with an apprehensive eye.
The reason I got as mad as hell
and on this subject continue to dwell
is because I really do care
and a good life with him I want to share.
I will not settle for any less
than each day of our lives together with happiness.
I advise him not to settle either,
even if it means we need a little breather.
We both must change in certain ways
if we want to rebuild a relationship that stays.
I know that I must come up higher
where it's brighter, lighter, and I have more desire,
but he must also come down lower
off his high horse, so we can take things slower.
We can't align on either persons weakest level
if a great relationship is where we want to revel.
I wish that he could just help me
by extending his hand and being able to see
that I can't be up when I'm feeling low,
and if he sees a better way to just let me know

Wendy DiBella

but not with annoyance in his tone;
only love can lift me out of that zone.
I wish that I could also help him
understand the reason I've gone out on a limb.
I know if we truly saw the perspective of the other
we could align in a neutral place with one another.

Reconnecting

For the first time we could both hear and see
that you can only change you and I can only change me.
In every disagreement we were BOTH so wrong,
fighting hard to change the other by standing our ground,
being strong.
But the one conversation that came from a different angle
where we saw our own emotional *nots* to untangle.
The realization that I had continuously accused you
of the things I was doing but could not see from my view.
And knowing all the times that you accused me
of the things *you* were doing wrong and angrily.
But none of that matters anymore;
this moment of reveal ended the cold war.
Once we knew it was all just habit and fear
that made accusations that were harsh or severe.
Once we saw each other's point of view,
the truth about ourselves we finally knew.
Once we looked *in* instead of looking out
we each became the change we wanted to see,
we turned our *in*-sight out.

Wendy DiBella

Realigned

I bought some new clothes to wear today;
I can remember the last time I felt this way.
We used to read riddle books and play Connect Four,
so I bought those too; we've been playing some more.
We've broken free from our disagreeing ways.
We're spending time just enjoying our days,
laughing out loud, giving reassuring glances,
appreciating each other as our relationship advances.
We happen to be really good together,
and we proved we can handle any weather.
I'm seeing now that it is a must
to live in the present and each other trust.
Trust you have each other's best interest at heart,
trust that difficult times don't have to tear you apart.
Trust that if two people who love each other lose their way,
they can align and come together to get it back any day.

Insight 16

Education

Student

No

Education

College is the cheapest cost
of monies spent, education sometimes lost.
Your teacher is the life you live
and learning is through what you give.
You will pay blood, sweat, and tears
and continually learn throughout the years.
When you give the best of you,
it comes back in multiples of two.
When it's money that you share,
you'll get back more than what's fair.
When you give out happiness and love,
you get back grace from above.
Out of all lessons the most valuable one taught
is that time cannot be earned or bought.

Wendy DiBella

Student

A student of life we all appear to be,
required to take courses in anatomy.
Learning about ourselves, gaining knowledge
and being tested just like in college.
We must learn how our bodies deal
so that we can obtain the tools to heal.
Connected together we all are,
challenged to continually raise the bar.
Different teachers we are afforded;
the world is the school in which we are boarded.
Some are held back, required to repeat a course.
Some skip forward, lesson need not be reinforced.
All of us are excited to graduate
so we can use what we learn to make our lives great.

No

Disappointment is frequently associated with the word *no*,
but actually it's a great word that helps you to be safe and grow.
If every light used for traffic control was set to stay on green,
you could imagine the collisions and damage of that scary scene.
No doesn't have to have a reason or explanation;
when you accept it at face value it's a source of liberation.
On the other hand if all the lights were always set to red
there would be no reason to get up or get out of bed.
Alternating stop and go get you to your destination
but it's the *no* that allows the space for mindful hesitation.
There really is a profound lesson for accepting and letting go;
it's taught and offered every time you get or give a resounding *no*.

Wendy DiBella

Insight 17

Health

Nutrition

Beauty

Health

Health is good condition of the body and the mind
a state of well-being that you measure in kind.
It's not that a healthy person never gets depressed;
it's just that when they do it's a brief momentary regress.
Even a healthy person may sometimes get sick,
but should they fall ill, they bounce back real quick.
Another sign of health is having great boundaries
with food, money, relationships, and all other sundries.
Health is the balance between high and low;
in laughter and inner beauty your health does show.
Health is the means to a greater end;
prioritize your health, and on that do not bend.

Nutrition

Nutritionally speaking you are what you eat;
on a cellular level only whole foods complete.
Improper eating always leads to starvation;
whether over- or underweight, it's harsh sensation
prevents you from having energy or thriving.
Lack of nutrients traps you in the mode of just surviving.
Your metabolism determines your level of health;
a great metabolic rate moves you with stealth,
creating the energy output required
so burning fat, exercise, and mental clarity is acquired.
Eating proper nutrients is the master key
that opens the door to being healthy.
There are areas of your body only nutrients can reach;
they protect, flush, or fill and prevent any breach.
Accessing optimal health and changing your current condition
metamorphically happens with a metabolic transition.
The significance of your diet cannot be overstated:
food is actually medicine and can provide the life you've awaited.

Beauty

"Beauty is only skin deep" is not a truthful saying;
the message that it sends is very poorly relaying
the truth about a person's attractiveness.
The effect and causes of their beauty is remiss.
Beauty actually comes from very deep within;
it radiates out and lights up the surface of your skin.
Skin, hair, nails, and glistening eyes all rely on this.
It's beauty's best kept secret, joy and happiness.
The weight of a person's stored fat cells
holds the anger and unhappiness in which a person dwells.
Beauty is in the eye of the beholder, we all seem to agree,
but inner beauty that shines out speaks universally.

Wendy DiBella

Insight 18

Yoga

Poker

Music

Yoga

Yoga is a luxurious sport;
from a place of closed mindedness it can't be learned or taught.
It requires that you be open enough
to show up in class and reveal all your stuff—
damage you are ready to face and heal—
people think it's stretching but that's not the deal.
Yoga is about folding and unfolding in space and time
the shortest distance to health and a life sublime.
When yoga is done with good form and measure,
your nervous system has space and is free from pressure.
Your body is your organs' home;
the practice involves your mind so it does not roam.
Organs like furniture go where there's room;
great form allows great function as you might presume.
Mentally and physical you will be in great shape:
taut on the outside, softer on the inside, and mentally escape.
Yoga is not a workout; it's a work in.
The rest you'll learn in class; it's time to begin.

Wendy DiBella

Poker

Poker is a game of skill,
strategy, timing, luck, and will
you win depends on you—
believing you can see it through.
Be quiet and listen to what others think;
this skill alone takes you to the brink
of using magic to win your game
by manipulating luck and creating a frame
that you simply insert your picture in
boasting your collection of chips, envisioning your win.
The main focus is not the cards in your hand;
its great timing and knowing your luck you command.
It's knowing that what you truly hold
are not just cards but skilled control.
Besides being great at the hands you play,
know the ones you lay down usually save the day.
To make the right moves that benefit you,
you must have the belief to know all this is true.
Make a date to meet yourself at every final table
and simply show up ready, willing and able.

Music

Take note of music's amazing gift:
it creates an internal harmonic shift.
Your kidneys are connected to your ears,
and that is a dialog about your fears.
Depending on what you're hearing or listening to
determines the emotional effect it has on you.
Music is read in the language of notes
that can lift you high and let you float
above the troubles in your mind,
allowing you to be present and unwind,
reminding you of past times that were fun.
Music is nostalgic and healing for everyone.

Wendy DiBella

Insight 19

Grateful

Letting Go

Happiness

Grateful

When you feel great and full of life,
like the happiness of a new man and wife,
the excitement of getting your first new car,
taking a road trip, traveling far.
Eating foods that you enjoy.
Getting a job, being employed.
Smelling a flower, reading a book.
Watching a movie, loving to cook.
Being grateful for everything you already have.
Basically, spending your time being glad.
Realizing the things you don't have are also a blessing
allow your gratitude to be continually expressing.
What you appreciate, appreciates, this fact is true:
say "thank you" every day; bring a greater, fuller life to you.

Wendy DiBella

Letting Go

When you feel safe, you can let go;
this is not necessarily what most people know.
If you are hanging off a cliff
you can only let go unless and if
something secure takes hold of you
that you know can bring you to safety, too.
If you are dangling way up high,
you can't let go; it's not safe to fly.
If you believe you are being judged,
you can't let go of feeling begrudged.
If you know that others mean you well,
you'll feel safe to share, confide, and tell.
When you know you don't feel safe within,
change what you must, so you can begin
feeling safe and secure; it's the only way
to let go of anything you'd like to release today.

Happiness

Always happy as can be
even when things were hard for me.
Always grateful for the kind
love and laughter in this life of mine.
Always thankful for what I've got,
never minding what I've not.
My family, I most appreciate;
they are truly amazing, supportive and great.
This is just to go and show
that life can be tough, but you should know
when the glass half full is what you see,
from your hardships you'll be free.

Wendy DiBella

Insight 20

Shame

Secrets

Speaking

Shame

Tapping in really lets it out.
Add articulations to scream and shout.
When being silent is your game
the end result cannot be fame.
Stating what is really true
and using it so it can't use you.
Not being afraid to let it flow
is the way to let it go.
Facing it is the only way
to move past fear of Judgment Day.
Why had I been afraid to say
that I'd been lamed in many ways?
I am now so free to share
these facts that are true, I do dare.
For silence can be a painful place
but inside out it's filled with grace.

*See *Tapping*, page 189

Wendy DiBella

Secrets

I have finally exposed my darker hours
that had held back a good amount of my powers.
Making decisions that had repercussions
that were so upsetting there were no discussions.
Suffering silently, exploiting things that were good
with blame and shame for what went on in the hood.
You might not think of me
to have such a lofty diary,
but in the journey I have traveled
certain things have unraveled,
and with that I did not feel deserving
or give myself permission to be serving
myself the highest quality of the things
that I desired and with all that does bring.
But now I see that I was young
and acted upon what I spoke in tongue,
and that was meant for me to do,
I was a good person and that is true.
And now my heart is healed and content
knowing what happened helped me grow and was meant.

Speaking

It is your story to be told,
and if you wish, it will be sold.
If you can share with honesty all of your story
then you will receive and reveal all of its glory.

Insight 21

Damage

Healing

Damage

Transported here in a human craft,
early damage was my draft.
I fell down a flight of stairs
which tore my aura that no one repaired.
It left a hole that made me leak
and made me vulnerable when others were bleak.
My tear was found by a new age healer
who explained that this type of damage is realer
than what most people are willing to believe.
That's why so many cannot receive
the health and happiness they so chase
that seems to plague the human race.
I'd like to prove that this is true
so you can apply it and be healed, too.
When you have issues and a doctor can't solve 'em
know it's not medical, it's a life problem.
Find energy healers that you can use
to participate in your well-being; infuse
new tools and methods towards making you well.
This is what I did and I hope you can tell
it healed and changed my life for the best.
It can do the same for you as well as the rest.

Wendy DiBella

Healing

How do you know if it's coming in or going out
with certainty beyond a shadow of a doubt?
When you experiencing an unpleasant intense feeling,
how do you know if it's newly created or you're healing?
You could be filing a new grievance in your draw,
or letting go of something old or painfully raw.
The key is to notice your relationship to it:
are you looking at it from above or engulfed in its pit?
When you are healing there's a pause in the thought
that keeps you from getting too overwrought.
You know you are healed when you simply feel great,
have faith, and distrust another mindset or state.
As long as you're prioritizing healing and love
and your actions fit these goals like a glove,
then you can trust, not only are you safe and in good hands
but you're directly connected to your important role in God's plans.

SECTION III

Insight 22

Traveling

Religion

Faith

Traveling

Words are the way to decode
life's many road signs while traveling this road.
Articulations the universe speaks through
mapping, gas, and rest stops to go to.
Know that when you're traveling far
you must be able to rely on your car.
You can't see where you're going if windows are dirty.
There's no joy in driving with flat tires, not sturdy.
You can't get far with fumes in your tank;
you will get lost if your road map is blank;
you will be safe if you stay in your lane;
and know where all your blind spots remain.
For we don't get hit by what we see coming
and that is why you have to be so cunning.
Rubbernecking will just slow you down;
focusing on others issues isn't very sound.
How you deal with traffic definitely brings
awareness to you of how you handle all things.
If you find that you need a tow,
let others help carry you to where you need to go.
If you find that you are lost,
ask for help and a road map no matter the cost.
I like to drive something rich, sleek, and smooth.
I like to have fun and listen to music that soothes.
Even an old car can be made a classic
with a high-end value and look fantastic.
A small car be great on gas,
fit in small spaces, get you there fast.
A beat-up car can be completely refurbished
with new parts and a paint job; you would be astonished.
Just in case you don't know it yet
your car reflects you: which one will you get?

Wendy DiBella

Religion

Religion speaks in many tongues;
its main purpose is to teach the young,
that all should succumb to a higher power
and follow good rules hour by hour.
Uniting in purpose can be a beautiful thing,
but individuals must remember to be accounting
to their true values built in when they're born
and minding their actions when decisions are torn.
Even though a religious belief may be true,
it's interpreted by a human, not necessarily you.
So make sure next time you act in "good faith,"
you have checked with your own values and asked if it's safe.

Faith

Faith is believing in something so strongly,
trusting in good even when things go wrongly.
It's not about going to temple, mosque, or church,
so for a greater good you continue to search.
It's not about being led by your nose
to follow the beliefs that others propose.
It's not about looking for safety in numbers
from people making unsafe blunders.
It's not about practicing faith in a place
and yet when at home fearing, not having grace.
It not about being convinced or converted
that to fear G-d you should be alerted.
It's believing in things you can't see or touch
and never having the need to hold, grip, or clutch.
It's about believing there exists a greater good,
and things come to you in the time that they should.
It's believing that the blind *can* see
and that not with everything should you agree.
It's believing you are safe and protected
and to your purpose already connected.
It's practicing faith everywhere you go
by not allowing fear to exist or grow.
It's connecting to the values deep in your soul
using skill and measure, so your actions you control.
It's knowing that it's *you* who has to choose,
good or bad and each time win or lose.
It's knowing overall that you reap what you sow
and your lessons can be learned quickly or slow.
In *awe* of the awesome it's easy to believe,
in the light of true greatness everything you can achieve.

Wendy DiBella

Insight 23

Armor

Jealousy

Judgment

Armor

A suit of armor is built to suit
your destiny and life's pursuit.
No one's armor fits on you;
you're unique in stature and colored hue.
When you try to try on theirs,
the weight and bulk on you wears.
Unnaturally uncomfortable two coats of armor are;
take theirs off, say, "au revoir."
You alone should only bear
the medal of honor *you* were given to wear.

Do not try to take on others' good fortune or burdens.
Your build and make up is designed especially to handle you,
the experiences and life that you are meant to have.

Wendy DiBella

Jealousy

Jealousy is believing someone else's something should be yours.
Pain is what is felt from the newly open sores
when thoughts of envy weigh in, making your decisions
causing rifts in relationships; animosity creates divisions.
No good could ever come from covetously thinking,
chances of obtaining what you covet, rapidly shrinking.
Insecurities that run deep with convincing convictions
become obstacles in your path, blockages and restrictions.
Strong belief that you're lacking in these aspects of your life
rip, shred, and cut you up with your own hunting knife.
If you wish to have the things that make *their* grass look greener
remember with that comes the rest of *their* life and demeanor.
What you have and how you're built is suited just for you,
precisely set to keep you on course and see *your* destiny through.
The only thing that you should look to with passion and desire
is the life you already have, solely, and in its entire.

Judgment

You're the judge, the jury, and the bailiff, too;
the courtroom drama hinges on what you decide to do.
Are you looking and listening for reasonable doubt
so life sentences you don't wrongfully give out?
Do you even really want to be
the only vote and person in the jury?
If you reserve judgment for the big man upstairs
then you won't be burdened with splitting so many hairs.
Each verdict in which you acquit or convict
is the future for yourself that you've just picked.

Wendy DiBella

Insight 24

Unconscious

Emotion

Sinking

Unconscious

When you do things you do not know
life's unconscious on the go,
and then one day you see it all,
and you can't help but feel appalled;
it's you who must effect a change,
so now you have to rearrange
the way you see and act and do
and bring a good life back to you.

Wendy DiBella

Emotion

Emotion is the key to this:
remove negativity so you can feel the bliss
so enwrapped in what you do
not knowing that it makes you blue.
Rise above the chattering mind
learn to yourself, to be kind;
use *tapping* every single time
negative feelings enter your mind.
Say this affirmation every day:
"I am joyful and carefree" and be on your way
to watching what's stored move out of you
get out of your way so you can love what you do.

*See *Tapping*, page 189

Sinking

Trapped in emotion
I was filled with devotion
but I didn't have a notion
of how to swim across this ocean.
Filled with fear of drowning
I was prevented from crowning
myself with a new life
free of trouble and strife.
Learning how to swim with skill
feels better than a numbing pill.
When I learned to kick, stroke, breathe,
in equal parts, I swam with ease.
My terror turned to joy so fast
that now I can swim out oh so vast.

Wendy DiBella

Insight 25

Present

Integrate

Present

To bring yourself to be here, in the now
unconscious thinking you must not allow.
Body, mind, and spirit must be connected
in order to find where you're being affected.
Scan your body on the left and right;
look for pain and muscles both loose and tight.
Think of each body part totally relaxed;
notice the difference in the parts that feel taxed.
When you find an area that is dense,
imagine a white light surrounding it like a fence.
Let the muscle melt in the warmth of the light
and keep repeating until all body parts feel right.
Anytime you notice your mind start to drift,
come back to your present; it is the greatest gift.

Wendy DiBella

Integrate

Integrate means to make a whole
or be woven into a part of your soul.
When you are ready to become one
in your narrative thread, first intertwine fun.
Two words that then must combine forces
are *integrity* and *greatness*, the energy sources.
Used together time and again
they provide the power to integrate in.
Integrity is the integral part of doing your personal best
to connect to your absolute greatness; use spirit and zest.

Insight 26

Fold

Passion

Inspiration

Fold

The shortest distance between two points is really just a fold.
A straight line is what you were taught; this thought you must remold.
There are no straight lines in nature; everything has a twist.
To know this truth enables you to start to get the gist.
Take a paper, paint a dot, and then fold it in half;
that dot will quickly reach the other side of your graph.
A fold in the space time continuum would allow time travel,
but it's better if we don't go there so the world we don't unravel.
Origami represents the highest level of precision
of creating any three dimensional form you can envision.
Flowers unfold gracefully as they grow and bloom,
unfolding to the magic of scents we use to make perfume.
Taking something flat and making it spherical
is nothing short of folding's unprecedented miracle.

Wendy DiBella

Passion

Passion is the driving force
fueled by power from your highest source.
It is what creates a creation
stemming from an inspired revelation.
To access the feeling of true passion
rise above concepts that require ration.
Open your valves and channel in
what would excite you from deep within,
be it thoughts of fortune, quiet joy, or being spry.
Let yourself be open to connect to passion's high.
Whether dancing, doing laundry or making your bed,
add some passion, as a common thread.
When you put passion into everything you do
you'll find presence and joy and experience the real you.

Inspiration

I watched a motivational speech by Vishen Lakhini.
I thought to myself, "Wow, he's so dreamy,"
but not the high school crush-on kind,
the dreams that make your world sublime.
Find out who inspires you,
and simply emulate what they do.

Wendy DiBella

Insight 27

Responsibility

Prioritize

Just Bee

Responsibility

What is your response-ability?
To notice and remove all hostility?
To use an appropriate amount of speed and agility
when heightening your performance and civility?
There is only one thing you're responsible for:
Putting love into action, love yourself to your core.

Wendy DiBella

Prioritize

Prioritize your routine, implement it every day;
work, relax, breath, laugh, live, love, and play.
Don't regret yesterday; don't worry about tomorrow;
focus on today's events, more time you cannot borrow.
Your daily routine defines the lines that keep
determining if you're high or low, shallow or deep.
Remember, what you put first, puts you first;
always drink lots of water to quench your thirst.
Use great boundaries, flow on through,
enjoying the details of your daily to do.
Watch and listen for the subtle clues;
look for miracles; don't you snooze.
When your day is prioritized like this,
your life is filled with laughter and bliss.

Just Bee

The balance now is clear to see,
a bee can sting, yet makes honey.
To some the sting hurts just a bit,
to others, a serious allergic fit.
All in all, the bee's own fate,
commences on its stinging date.
But in the act of sweetening its hive,
it knows all the joy of being alive.

Wendy DiBella

Insight 28

Moms

Children

Woven

Moms

Moms do come in different forms;
to their child's life they do their best to conform.
Teaching, learning from each day
for their child's health and happiness they frequently pray.
Looking at, thinking of what to do next—
the role of a mother is pretty complex:
reaching and striving to give their all,
holding their children up so they can feel tall.
Safety and security they work hard to give
so a blessed life the child can live.
Some moms have the tools to provide
the best solutions for the children they guide.
Some moms had no example to lead from
and have to wing whatever circumstances do come.
Each mom's mothering is vastly unique;
a smart child will learn from the best and worst of their technique.

Wendy DiBella

Children

Children are a gift from God
stemming from your roots, grown from sod.
They are sent to teach and learn the way
to do things better, enrich your day.
To connect, thrive, and grow together,
requires that you follow this to the letter:
Give them the highest quality of things
while providing the best you, you can bring.
Substitution is not an option
with the exception of adoption.
Take care of your health for that is required
to keep them in good health and always inspired.
Your children will know if you are lying;
they are also affected by everything you're buying.
If you're simply aware of what you're doin'
together you will undo history's ruin.
Be honest with them and pay close attention:
if you listen, they will always take time to mention
what exactly they require from you
so their very best they can be and do.

Woven

Woven into each string of my narrative thread;
my body, soul, mind, and head.
The fibers made of pure, light stitching,
the reason my life is so enriching:
The connected, integrated internal clock
eternally ticks in time with the offspring of my flock.
With acceptance, radiance, and love we click
together, in a rhythmic tic tic tic.

Wendy DiBella

Insight 29

Challenges

Comfort

Can't

Challenges

Challenges can be hard to face;
all people are challenged to embrace
the situations that fill their lives.
A challenge-free life is for what we all strive,
but in fact the circumstances that do arise
give us insight and open our eyes.
They help us learn to deal and grow
and obtain information that before we didn't know.
Use the experiences you face today
to gain a new perspective that you can take away.
Apply what you learned and now know
to be free of the challenge you were given to grow.

Wendy DiBella

Comfort

Staying in your comfort zone
prevents progressing on your own.
Doing things that may feel right
but leave you tired and uptight.
Get out of your comfort zone
so you can see where you are prone
to living in same old, same old
instead of reaching for the gold.
You have to be much more efficient
in *tapping* the areas you are deficient.
It's not so comfortable at all
continually contributing to your fall.
Confusing demands that are weak
will not bring you what you seek.
If your actions match your truth
you can feel the joy of youth.
Make certain statements crystalline
and fill your life with every dream.

*see *Tapping*, page 189

Can't

Can't lives on won't street
in a town called lonely.
With residence like Never, Don't, Should've, and If Only.
Since you can choose where you want to live,
move into "Yes I Can" town for all it has to give.

Wendy DiBella

Insight 30

Pity

Betrayal

Anger

Flawed

Pity

They say the blind can only see
the vision of a greater thee.
I think I now know that is true
as my eyes are closed
my rhymes flow through
so do not pity anyone's life;
it is never what reflects their strife.

Wendy DiBella

Betrayal

The pain was from an icy pick
made of water, a frozen stick.
Cuts so smooth and cuts so deep,
the pain was harsh; it made me weep.
Attacker was so smart and cunning
his weapon melted, he was off and running
from the truth that he was mean,
his acts of kindness were very lean.
The silence made an awful sound;
it shattered spirits to the ground.
When confronted on his action,
he was very puzzled with little reaction.
He had made his defense just to say,
"I'd never hurt you in any way."
He had seen no proof of his attack;
he didn't know he stabbed me in the back.
Until it became too much for him to deny
and he was able to see it with his own eyes.
From that wound we finally did heal
and more than that we learned a great deal.

Anger

When only anger fills your heart
with sticky black tar that won't come apart.
When anguish stems from anger's root
and thoughts of something you might shoot.
At the bottom of that blackened pit
you start to give in, you give up, and you sit.
Your head is heavy; your chin is down;
not enough energy to muster a frown.
And then a rope thus does appear
and you think, "Oh just leave me here."
But someone on the other end
is insistent; they just won't bend.
They say, "Come on just grab the rope,"
but you're so at the end of it you just can't cope.
You can't hold on tight enough
to be hoisted up; it's just too tough.
So the rope ascends, you prepare to die,
but a noise startles you from up high,
and before you know what happens next,
the rope descends with a man and a vest.
He straps you into the vest he brought;
you're in his arms; he's got you caught.
As you're lifted towards the light,
you feel his love; it's going to be alright.

Wendy DiBella

Flawed

When you are floored by someone's flaws
and broken are the very last of your straws.
Laying down, in full review
of all the ways they have hurt you
is exactly when you must choose
to love them the most, not necessarily excuse
the actions they took in which they made a mistake.
Let loving them, regardless, be the action *you* take.
Only when you can love someone who has done wrong
will you fully love yourself and live heart strong.

Insight 31

Advice

Good/Bad

Achievement

Advice

To give advice on troubles and life
first overcome your own difficulties and strife.
By having a higher awareness and being able to see
what goes on all around you, a view of 360 degrees.
By taking the advice you've given out so far
you can be in a better place than *you* currently are.
For if you can do what you know others should
and take your own advice for your own greater good,
then no one would actually need advice from you.
When you lead by example others emulate what you do.

Wendy DiBella

Good/Bad

Maybe it's good or maybe it's bad;
it's hard to tell when confused, mad, or sad.
What if it happened for your greater good
and it's directing you in the direction it should?
What if it leads to bigger and better
like when less is more, in a to-the-point letter?
What if you're just meant to have the experience
and it's for the growth of your soul's existence?
What if they are signs screaming "dead end"—
are you able to heed them and turn the bend?
What if the feelings are just so you can feel
what its like to live, be you, be real?
What if the things that you dislike the most
are what you need to embrace so through life you can coast?
What if it all was just your thoughts, like a dream
and you weren't falling apart at every seam?
What if no judgment was decreed at each turn
and instead there was acceptance with a lesson to learn?
What if you saw that it is neither or both,
and your power choose gives you the greatest growth.

Achievement

If my words help you see a way
to heal your pain, to save your day,
then I have received what I have asked
to know the peace, love, and joy that is so vast,
and what that means is you may too
achieve the dreams you have in you.

Wendy DiBella

Insight 32

Tiredness

Numbness

Feelings

Tiredness

Tired of feeling tired and defeated?
Lacking luster, faith has fleeted?
Inner vibrance shutting down?
Facial expression, not a smile or a frown?
This type of tired is mental exhaustion;
it's your body waving a sign of caution.
That you are dwelling way too much,
negative thoughts in your mind, do not clutch.
Fear, anxiety, and depression play a role;
think of them like an espionage mole.
Any thoughts of future or past
remove from your mind; do not let them last.
Mind chatter is not the fuel to use
when making everyday decisions in choices you choose.
Get energy from a different source;
only the present moment teaches this course.
Think and act based on living in the now,
and any other influences, disallow.

Wendy DiBella

Numbness

The numbness that happens when your legs are crossed
is a break in the circulation, a blood flow loss.
There's a pinch, a pressure, a restriction, a block
up until the time you uncross to unlock.
Feeling emotionally numb is no different;
it's about being crossed, the experience is referent.
When nothing is flowing in or out,
numbness happens, to alert you, no doubt.
Numbness doesn't mean you lose your head or legs,
but really you should listen to your body when it begs.
Letting yourself feel so you don't deny
the feelings that are real and sometimes make you cry
because when you bury them deep down inside
at some point you'll feel crossed, no longer able to hide
the difficult experiences that you don't want to feel.
They'll keep coming up, you're not supposed to conceal.
They are meant to be seen, heard, and felt
instead of suppressed, denied, and dwelt.
At the point they take up too much room
numbness happens from excessive gloom.
It's safer to face it, feel it, and let it flow
than to hold it down, as it builds up, making you low.
When there's flow once again there's a tingling sensation
and that is your sign of your rising vibration.

Feelings

Feelings are the ultimate clue
of how to gauge what you should do.
Feeling down is a waving red flag
that lets you know you have an energy lag.
In every moment that you think you are lacking
you're basically sending all your dreams packing.
We all know that the goal is to feel good
but how to do that can be misunderstood.
It's not about waiting for specific life changes
so that from upset to happy your feeling exchanges.
It's not about fixing frustrations or fighting;
it's all about what you are feeling and inviting.
It's knowing scientifically that the laws of attraction
govern, rule, and are based on your reaction.
You are a magnet, like attracts like;
when you focus on problems it brings more dislike.
Contrary to that, when your feelings are high
great things come to you, limited not even by the sky.
Feeling badly brings whatever you're trying to avoid.
Happy feelings pull in things that make you overjoyed.
Change the way you react to your unwanted conditions
by focusing on positive feelings and desired acquisitions.
Summon the feeling of how you would feel
if you were living your dream life, and it was all real.
Hold on to that feeling for at least eighteen seconds;
to your life all good things this technique beckons.
These instructions positively change your energy flow
and create the feelings and conditions you've been longing to know.

Wendy DiBella

Insight 33

Wanting

Having

Doing

Wanting

Wanting's closest relatives are yearning, wishing, hoping,
all of whom have no life and just get on by coping.
Hunting and looking for things just out of reach
strongly clasping onto hope, emulating a leech.
Demanding the presence of things they desire
from poverty and desperation seeking what they admire.
They all are very different from Goals and Vision;
they lack luster and have no plan of skill, pursuit, or precision.
What they want is not ever what they get
because they vibrate in perpetual feelings of upset.
Wanting is tricky in the way it does deceive
you into believing what you want is what you need.
Together they all create a chain reaction
that has no end and provides no satisfaction.
Once you see them clearly, simply don't take their bait,
and you'll automatically live and thrive in a positive, satiated state.

Wendy DiBella

Having

Having's closest relatives are did it, got it; great
things come to you when living in this vibrational state.
Having comes from feeling that it's already yours
that sensation emanates out through your very pores.
It's vital to know what you feel is what you shall attract
when you create a positive feeling, in your favor cards are stacked.
What you get is based on what you believe you can;
this fact is true; it's easy to do and makes life better than
thinking and dwelling on a low vibration based on what you lack
because all that does is bring in things that continue to hold you back.
The Haves and Have Nots are separated by a single thread;
the Haves believe their dreams are real
and the Have Nots live in dread.
To move out of the Have Not lane, just make a sharp right turn
and follow the road called Happiness and having will return.

Doing

Knowing and doing are two different things;
until that's understood, the confusion bell rings.
Don't let your mind trick you into thinking
that just because you know it, your action is linking.
Thoughts seem real, too real sometimes,
and that is when the confusion bell chimes.
You know what to do—you are a good person—
so why is it happening to you, that what you dislike seems to worsen?
It's only because simply knowing it alone
is not enough to lift you out of a zone.
You must actually *do* all these things you know,
the advice you give, without resistance, just flow.
When doing this, two major things fall into place:
participation in your well-being and connection with the human race.

Wendy DiBella

Insight 34

Now

Peace

Purpose

Now

What does it mean to live in the "now"?
It's a slower pace than life's race does allow.
To current activity mind connects and understands
and it happily moves at the pace of your hands.
Where you are right now is where you choose to be.
This present state of pace is your grace guarantee.

Wendy DiBella

Peace

Peace is where all the pieces fall into place
embodying a whole, connectivity's embrace,
higher selves integrated on lower plains
mindful understandings, beyond our brains.
The power of energy's gentle pace.
A calm inner smile, emptied space.
Tranquility, repose, serenity and quietude
with no cloaks of armor, comfortably bare, nude.
A silent acceptance, with no judgements to boot.
It's how you come in; in your birthday suit.

Purpose

There is no difference between a purpose or dream:
both are designed for you soul's regime.
It's so simple, hidden in plain sight.
I'll give you a hint—it's not the things you fight.
The areas where you struggle are there to show
you exactly where it is you're not supposed to go.
But what speaks from a higher place, in a lower tone
is the purpose or dream that from now on should be known.
Look for the moments when you feel at peace,
when happiness or joy within you seems to increase.
Notice what you are doing right there and then,
that allowed you to have that moment of Zen.
Give some space for the realization to grow
that you have found your purpose and now you know.

Wendy DiBella

Insight 35

Pattern

Permission

Signs

Pattern

The pattern woven into these Articulations
reflects worldly patterns and their vibrations.
All are created to heighten your mood
and provide a nutritious dialog of food.
The pattern in life appears everywhere;
once you learn it, it's easy to conform and prepare
because when you know what comes next;
there is no guess work; you don't feel perplexed.
From summer turns fall then winter then spring,
water flows over rocks instead of resisting.
From morning comes midday then evening then night;
life is good when you choose being happy over right.
From light to dark then from dark back to light,
nothing remains permanently, pitch black or bright.
From birth to death and death to rebirth
keeps you grounded, always coming back down to earth.
Expansion and contraction, ebb and flow,
reflect holding on and letting go.
Every single day the earth is enlightened by the sun,
sun takes nothing in return, showing how selflessness is done.
Everything has pattern; just follow the design
before you know it, you and your purpose will align.

Wendy DiBella

Permission

No specific permission will be granted
for you to have a life enchanted.
Do not wait for the approval of others
not friends, or colleagues, or siblings or mothers.
The signs you seek will not appear
as marching bands with flags and cheer.
Instead the signs are not that subtle;
you're shown the way in each rebuttal.
It's when you stop resisting things
and instead fill your time as would kings.
Experience and indulge in simple luxuries;
dub yourself worthy of joyful activities.
Only you can give yourself security clearance
and authorize a wonderful life using great perseverance.

Signs

Sometimes we don't realize our train tracks have crossed;
we don't notice the signs; we don't look for the moss.
Then all of a sudden a sign appears
that says, "Wrong Way" and evokes our fears.
All this time you've been traveling along
listening to music, singing your favorite song,
but then in a single instance of time
your perception changes; it turns on a dime.
You now realize that it's not what you thought;
the place you're headed is not where you ought.
This insight puts a decision to you,
make a hard right and your highest self pursue?
Or do you keep going straight pretending it's not true
that you've misunderstood what is best for you?
Will you let your gut feeling come right up in front?
Or do you stay on this course and continue to hunt?
Will you let the inner voice of reason that's distant and low
become the beacon of light that guides you with glow?
Get over the fact that you spent so much time
going out of the way of your ideal life that's prime.
Be smart, choose the path that will lead you right to
your dreams and your purpose; they're waiting for you.

Wendy DiBella

Insight 36

Support

Suicide

Help

Support

A stable foundation is the greatest support;
it's not an area you want to fall short.
In life always start from the ground up
to progress from this spot in which you have wound up.
To have a great support system, you want to ensure,
only lean on things that are safe and secure.
Support is available to you from all around;
it takes a village to help you well round.
Don't lean on your lower back for support;
use the strength of your feet and your legs to transport.
In order to stand something up erect,
use a right angled book end to perfect.
Knowing where support *is* and *is not*
gives you access to what you need in exactly the right spot.

Wendy DiBella

Suicide

I will not give you up for dead.
I've heard the things that you have said.
You are hurt from your beliefs;
I wish I had power to give you relief.
God helps those who help themselves
and sees the good above all else.
Many things formed our lives this way,
but there's still a chance to save the day.
I'd never give you up for dead;
please don't believe the thoughts in your head.
For I remember so much good
that brought us close, as it should.
It's just that I feel like you can't see
that I'm right here and I'm still me.
It's hard to watch you be so sad—
It breaks my heart and makes me mad.
Every day I think of you
and if there is anything I can do
that can bring us to the present day
and wipe all your painful memories away.
Today we have a chance to change,
to make amends and heal the pain.
You have great skills, can't you see?
The blessings you have can set you free.
Can you focus on good things that you have
so that you will not feel so sad?
There is no peace if you are gone;
stay with us and let's move on.
Believe my truth that I really care,
I LOVE YOU AND THE WORLD NEEDS YOU HERE!

I am writing down all the things I truly love and admire about you,
for you to know that you are worthy, special, valuable, and loved too.

Help

When you can't fix it by yourself,
use the skills of someone else.
Others can see where you are stuck;
it's not because you have bad luck.
Trust: they'll show you what to do;
reach out—now your time is due.

Wendy DiBella

Insight 37

Tree

Timing

Time

Tree

A tree has texture, depth, and dimension;
giving and peaceful existence is its intention.
Oxygen, shade, great timing, and shelter
is every tree's offer when the sun makes you swelter.
Colored leaves fall when the wind blows
to signal you to change your clock and your clothes.
As it gets cold it gives you wood to make a fire;
its warmth, glow, and effort you appreciate and admire.
When it's time to come out and spring into action
beautifully new colored leaves are its source of attraction.
Every single season, seasons us all
with the flavors of life through each spring and fall.
So what can be gained from the study of a tree?
How to live life rooting, rising, and free.

Wendy DiBella

Timing

Timing is everything, to us all that is clear:
stocks picks, parties, having the right career.
It's not so important when equities are bought;
it matters when you sell, we learn and are taught.
When timing your parties for good turnout and fun
people mingle, make friends, find love, become one.
Seizing the opportunity of jobs offered or lost
if you trust in the timing, no signals get crossed.
When timing is good, all events fall in place;
ease and happiness in your life you embrace.
When timing is off, even just a little,
things are puzzling, like a difficult riddle.
To get your timing cues directly from heaven
all of your actions you must leaven,
rise to occasions, and slightly modify
the areas of your life that don't gel or fly.
Trust that your timing from above is well planned;
when you have faith in timing, it comes to you first hand.

Time

Manipulation of real time
requires cultured skills of mine.
If you don't like it, do it fast
and if you do, slow down; make it last.
These are not the skills we're taught;
we slow it down when we are wrought
and these are not the tricks we learn;
life stands still as we burn.
Love and money seem to flee
right past many so swiftly.
Know that it is in our power
to run right past our darkest hour
to make our currency flow and last
and manipulate how time is passed.
But knowing how to do just that
requires these skills that you use, stat.

Wendy DiBella

Insight 38

Skill

Tapping

Strengths/Weaknesses

Skill

Skill is the difference between terror and joy;
with good technique you can enjoy.
If you sail across the ocean skilled at sea
a storm will exhilarate you, make you feel free.
In contrast to that, a sailor with poor skills
in that same storm, will not feel those thrills.
A magician does not ever rely on luck;
neither should you when you are stuck.
When you know that you try really hard
and still can't pull out the exact right card,
go back and check your skills and technique
and do it again and again until you obtain what you seek.

Wendy DiBella

Tapping

Tapping into the part of you
that's strong and light and knows what to do
takes more than using just your brain
to undo damage and make you feel sane.
At the point that you are ready to let go,
add tapping to your repertoire. Here's what you need to know:
Simply look up online, find and see
professionals who are experts in EFT.
Emotion Freedom Technique is its name
and letting go of negativity is its fame.
To get the best results hire someone who
is a therapist or healer with tapping skills, too.
"Location, location, location's" importance is true,
where to do it, when to do it, and on what parts of you?
All of this information EFT has mapped out
when used correctly it removes negativity and doubt.
The art of tapping into this,
is the road to a life of happiness and bliss.

Strengths/Weaknesses

Strengths become your weaknesses, from when you are born
like the favorite couch that gets sat on gets worn.
It's better to be a paper cup that holds water
than a steel cup with a hole that leaks at its border.
If your strength is that you are very strong
then the peace of surrender at some point you will long.
If your strength is that you are good at debate
than arguing is the way to other people you'll relate.
If your strength is that you are extremely smart
then your mind and tongue at constant work will tax your heart.
Recognize your weaknesses, use them to strengthen
your experiences, so a good life you can lengthen.

Wendy DiBella

Insight 39

Future

Honesty

Wings

Future

Your future is determined by the direction
that you are facing now absent course correction.
Though no one knows exactly what the future holds,
common sense can dictate how things may unfold.
Taking your future into your own hands
is certainly doable if well planned;
you must know what you are shooting for
before you can expect to better your score.
To change your current trajectory
you have to implant a new directory
of targets that you would like to reach—
for instance, new things you may want to learn or teach.
Perhaps your goals and visions are a bit more ambitious—
like fame, a dream house, or something auspicious.
It can be anything and everything that with you strikes a chord;
all you must do to get started is write it down; create a vision board.

Wendy DiBella

Honesty

Honesty's most subtle cue,
you're not fooling me, I'm not fooling you.
Nothing is lying, not one little bit;
energy tells and will always admit.
Revealed are the clues that honestly inform
the truth in each glance, mannerism, and form.
The universe reads inner feelings to decide
what to your life it chooses to provide.
When you are happy, wholehearted, and true
many more blessings bestow on you.
When you pretend you're "grateful" or "great"
you may fool yourself but *it* won't take the bait.
People that know how to read energy,
just like the universe, can easily see
what you're feeling and thinking, your truth.
Honesty's vibration is the fountain of youth.
Over beauty, balance, and glow it has control.
Honesty strengthens the body, mind, and soul.

Wings

The coin to heads is now flipped up;
her wings spread wide from her golden cup.
She writes the words that right the wrong,
a singing bird of lovely song.
Pastries made of just white light,
she bakes to lighten up the night.
An angel of a newer kind,
of earthly soul, body and mind.
Here she lives, her life's begun,
she's suited to enjoy the fun.
All strings are gone, all life is good,
she's active in the neighborhood.
An angel on earth has appeared,
in human form, she is revered.
She didn't grow wings before she flew;
she leaped first and then they grew.

Wendy DiBella

Insight 40

You

Vision

Vibration

Words

Views

You

If you can't swim, you will sink down;
it's not the water's fault you drown.
It's not the weather forecasted to come;
it's whether or not you're dressed to be protected from
the elements that require certain skills
like proper gear when you're hiking up hills.
It's knowing what to do if there is a fire,
always having a spare to replace a flat tire.
It's drinking more water in altitudes up high
because that air is thin and dry.
It's not the hammer that hits the nail;
it's up to you what get's impaled.
It's not the event that makes you upset;
a negative reaction is the greatest threat.
Skill, technique, and preparation ensure
prevention, which is nine tenths of the cure.
Once you know that it's all in your hands,
obtain the knowledge necessary to make great plans.

Wendy DiBella

Vision

"A vivid mental image" is how we describe *vision*.
What that picture looks like is purely your decision.
People pay a lot so they can have an opportunity to see
beautiful views, picturesque paintings, things that give them glee.
If you knew your thoughts really do construct
manifestation of material possessions,
behavioral patterns and conduct,
would you be more careful when choosing colors and contrast?
Would you seek out impressions from where beautiful art is cast?
Would you fill your mind with all the things you wish
like health, happiness, love, success, or enjoying your favorite dish?
Can you start to see the picture painted here?
Is your mental image becoming much more clear?
Close your eyes, lift your chest and chin, tell me what you see?
Are you already on your way to being the next great visionary?

Vibration

Individual and collective levels of vibration
determine the feelings and experiences of every nation.
Feelings that create negative vibrations
manifest various levels of frustrations.
Feelings that create positive vibration
manifest higher levels of elation.
Thoughts create feelings, which are just sensations
based on negative or positive thought formations.
To vibrate and align with positive affirmations
you simply have to understand the thought-to-feeling relations.

Wendy DiBella

Words

The power of words is undeniable;
they are very consistent and extremely reliable.
One word or letter can change everything.
Your words dictate what your life does bring.
Love, Light, and Lord—is the *L* integrated and stirred
into *World,* which is created from its root, *word.*

The fun in this Articulation is that you get to figure out
that from the mighty "word" our "world" did sprout.

Views

I found a new way to heal the pain
something better to put in my vein.
Removing stuck emotions that run so deep
will start your body's good housekeep.
Insert daily gratitudes
to change your physical latitudes.
From a higher vantage point
your patience and vision can conjoint;
your will and your goals can meet there, too,
and embrace any positive point of view.
From higher up you can clearly see
positive changes happening gradually.

Wendy DiBella